WHAT CAN I DO TO HELP LAZARUS?

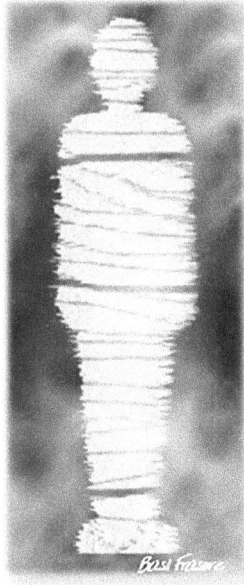

Reaching Out with Knowledge and Compassion to Survivors of Domestic Abuse in our Congregations

HARRIET I. COOK

ISBN 979-8-89112-333-5 (Paperback)
ISBN 979-8-89112-334-2 (Digital)

Copyright © 2024 Harriet I. Cook
All rights reserved
First Edition

Cover Image: Basil Frasure, PhD
www.wholeperson-counseling.org/
Used by permission

Scripture quotations marked "NKJV" are taken from the New King James Version®. Copyright © 1982 by Thomas Nelson. Used by permission. All rights reserved.

Scripture quotations marked "NASB" are taken from the (NASB®) New American Standard Bible®, Copyright © 1960, 1971, 1977, 1995, 2020 by The Lockman Foundation. Used by permission. All rights reserved. lockman.org"

All rights reserved. No part of this publication may be reproduced, distributed, or transmitted in any form or by any means, including photocopying, recording, or other electronic or mechanical methods without the prior written permission of the publisher. For permission requests, solicit the publisher via the address below.

Covenant Books
11661 Hwy 707
Murrells Inlet, SC 29576
www.covenantbooks.com

The author is not an expert in the field of abuse. She is sharing knowledge gained through relationships on some level with over a dozen abused wives, sharing experiences with some of those women, and continued education.

She does not deny that there are some male victims of female abuse or that occasionally a woman might make false accusations. However, her experiences have all been with women, the gender typically easier to prey upon. Therefore, feminine pronouns are used when speaking of the target, victim, or survivor.

It is her great hope that more Christians will come to recognize the devious tactics used by an abuser and the devastating effects upon the target. Her goal is to enlighten those in official and lay positions in our churches so that we can better minister Christ's love to those wounded by intimate partner abuse.

ENDORSEMENTS

After reading this booklet, I felt a sense of relief along with the thought that, finally, somebody understands. Now, people will believe me. By understanding and believing, I do not only mean the ability of others to conclude that I am not crazy but also the ability to comprehend the practicalities of getting out of an abusive relationship as clearly pointed out in this booklet. As much as abuse victims are living in an environment of fear and torment, it is an environment in which we know how to survive. The trauma we have suffered has rewired our brains to where we are convinced that the abusive environment we are living in is our natural habitat and it is what we deserve.

As human beings, we are made up of three parts: body, soul, and spirit. This booklet shines a bright light on each part and their unique individual needs. It tells you how you can help us heal our soul wounds, minister to us spiritually, and puts a much-needed emphasis on the economic and logistical challenges we face.

Wendelyn Hauch, Licensed Pastoral Counselor, NCCA

Harriet Cook has been in our lives since 1975 and is the most influential sister in Christ I have encountered. I believe this book is absolutely the inspiration Christ laid on her heart. The booklet *What Can I Do to Help Lazarus?* not only opened my eyes to the abuse that exists in our world today but gives insight into how we can love those and help those suffering in difficult relationships, whether the abused are women or men. I wish I had this years ago watching my son go through this abuse. The main influence here is to help those in need through the love of Christ. Sitting down to read a second time.

P. Means

I am very happy to endorse this booklet, *What Can I Do to Help Lazarus?* This project is important in an age when the works of darkness are becoming more pronounced and more insidious. There is sometimes a disconnect between the church and an understanding of the evil that is at work in our society. There needs to be some education about what some spouses go through, in trying to honor God and their marriage vows.

Galatians 5:1 NIV reads, "It is for freedom that Christ has set us free. Stand firm, then, and do not let yourselves be burdened again by a yoke of slavery." But what if the slavery is enforced by your spouse? The tormentor some-times fits the description from 2 Corinthians 11:13–14. "For such people are false apostles, deceitful workers, mas-querading as apostles of Christ. And no wonder, for Satan himself masquerades as an angel of light." They appear to be believers and are skilled at manipulation and deception. Harriet Cook's insight and compassion will bring revela-tion and wisdom to you as you seek to understand people locked into a nightmare marriage. You will receive scriptural guidance and come to understand the love of God for those in difficult situations.

My interaction with "Lazarus" began as a friend of the author, but I was also helping a close family member extricate themselves from a marriage that was not emotionally or spiritually healthy. They were devoted to their spouse and loved them, but it was becoming increasingly difficult to live with the abuse. Their own life and safety made it imperative to escape the daily torment. Harriet's insight brought relief that someone else could really understand what we were facing. The author could see through the carefully sculpted image that abusers craft. This brought comfort and clarification of the situation and helped us to realize that God was aware and was very present in the situation. Because of this personal connection, I am very glad that Harriet is making this material available to all those who want to help the Lord reach and minister to the brokenhearted.

A Friend, Author, and Bible Teacher

Luke 5:17–26 tells the story of a faith-filled group of friends who did what their paralyzed friend could not do for himself—make his way to Jesus through a dense crowd of people. Narcissistic abuse is paralyzing—crippling one with fear, doubt, confusion, and grief. On the path out of that abuse, one needs others to lead and guide them through the dark tunnel of narcissistic abuse and into the light and love of Christ and His healing Word.

I was that paralyzed (wo)man badly in need of being rescued, and God answered my desperate cries for help through His Word; Harriet's book, *What Can I Do to Help Lazarus?*; and my dear group of godly, praying friends. Filled with wisdom and practical help, "Lazarus" is a lifeline for those leaving narcissistic abuse. I was relieved that I did not walk that path alone but saddened that many others going through the very same thing do have to walk it alone. *What Can I Do to Help Lazarus?* is vital to help one through the process of unwrapping the grave clothes of abuse.

Stacy Jenkins

DEDICATION

Any accolades that might result from writing what the Lord has given to me are dedicated to the following:

- Our gracious and merciful Lord Jesus—the One Who never fails and the One Who walks with us through our deepest trials.
- My wonderful husband, Rick, who demonstrates Ephesians 5 daily. *From "I do" until now, I couldn't have walked this path without you and your unending love. I love you with all my heart.*
- My Sissy, who stayed faithful to the Lord in every way.
- The many women who are or have been abused in multiple ways by the men they trusted would love and cherish them while upholding their vows: men who covenanted with them before God, family, and friends.

CONTENTS

To the Reader

Pastors, counselors, leaders, and congregations—the Lord has placed me in a position to be a voice for the abused in our Houses of Worship and to bring into the light the many hidden aspects of spousal abuse. It seems that many of those in leadership have not been taught how abusers operate nor been encouraged to consider the whole counsel of God. I hope to help you identify the need, the cause, and how to care for the hurting hearts of the lambs you are shepherding as you defend against the wolves.

Suppose you are not in leadership but have discovered this little booklet while you are living in an abusive marriage. You might find some "aha!" moments that name what you have been enduring. Perhaps the thoughts and ideas presented here will help you as you take a stand against the evil being perpetrated against you. May these reflections assist you when you seek help from those in your life, whether they are Christian leaders or family members.

If you are courageously trying to keep sane in an abusive marriage, may I offer wisdom and encouragement from my sixty-four years of walking with Jesus.

- God sees you just as you are, and He loves you—no matter what.

- You are not responsible for your abuser's nefarious and ugly actions against you.
- You are *not* alone. Keep close to Jesus. Let Him hold you. Listen for His instructions.
- Jesus does not approve of anyone mistreating another; the Bible is full of God's attitude toward oppressors and His love for the oppressed.
- You *don't* deserve to be mistreated.
- You *are* worthy to be loved!
- Psalm 91 is perfect to memorize and declare out loud over yourself daily. Put it in the first person ("Because I dwell," etc.) perspective.
- If your cries for help are not respected in the church you attend, is there another local church whose leaders will listen with respect? Perhaps a search is in order?
- There is hope! I have witnessed miracles of provision God has sent. Cash gifts—sometimes the correct amount at the moment needed; firewood to keep warm; gifts such as shopping for necessary items; a new safe phone; pro bono licensed counseling; the "right" person speaking up and presenting facts in the face of intimidating lies; and biblical pastors that stood for women in the face of slander and threats; someone calling at *just the precise moment* to share the perfectly appropriate-for-the-moment, encouraging Bible verse the Lord impressed them with. I have witnessed too many occurrences of provision to recall them all!

I also know several ladies who sought the Lord, waited upon Him during their healing process, and are now happily married to the kindest, most amazing husbands. All is not lost, dear one. Make Jesus your sole authority, and lean into Him!

SPECIAL THANKS

- Jon McIntosh, our pastor who honorably stood with several women in our church walking through domestic abuse, even when he was daily harassed and slandered. Wendy McIntosh and Claire McIntosh, both staff pastors, whose gentle counsels were the voices, the wisdom, and the comfort of Jesus:
  Jon, Wendy, and Claire, it is with profound gratitude that we honor you for the care, compassion, and character you held and continue to exhibit. Thank you from the bottom of our hearts! We love you dearly.
- Our cherished Cook children and granddaughter, who lived in our home during some of these experiences:
  Hosanna, Aaron, Melody, Robby, Erika, and Briana, thank you for each and every instance when my mind was distracted and you graciously understood. You loved my Sissy as though she had been born to me and also to you. The compassion and kindness you showed her are not forgotten. I'm so grateful for the loving partners and grandchildren you have brought into our family. You each are loved more than my heart can express!
- Basil Frasure, PhD, cover artist:
  Your artistry is perfect! Thank you for allowing me to use your illustration.

- Kathy Spampinato, my editor:
  I am blessed by your friendship. I appreciate the skills and time you contributed. Thank you so much!

INTRODUCTION

Through relationship with acquaintances, friends, and family members, I can count fourteen to fifteen women I know who have walked the road of domestic abuse. I had the honor of walking with my special sister from another mother through a horrific case of malignant narcissistic domestic abuse, both pre-separation and post-emancipation.

Amid the time frame of Sissy's continual postdivorce harassment by her abuser, I manned our church phones each week during pastoral staff meetings. During one quiet Tuesday morning, I utilized my time studying John 11:39–44, the account of Lazarus. The Lord revealed a comparison of Lazarus to a woman escaping domestic abuse—faster than I could write!

God never wastes the challenges we walk through. He has compelled me to combine that Lazarus revelation with the experiences that I, my Sissy, and my husband encountered and to draw from the experiences of others we have known who walked a similar path to freedom.

As a wife, mother, and mother-in-law of US Marines, mother to three plus their spouses, and grandmother to five, I generally don't mince words. If I come across to you as bold (hopefully not offensive), please know this: I have the utmost love and respect for pastors. I have served under some of the very best for over fifty years! But I see so many holes in the fabric of the church at large when it comes to recognizing the evidence of abuse and caring for the wounded. Without the teaching of what to look for, how are we, as the Body of Christ, to rescue and help heal the abused?

The marriage covenant is something I believe in with all my heart. It is sacred! Those pledging to the promise are responsible before the Lord to keep their vows. But bilateral covenants, like legal contracts, are only as good as the faithfulness of *both* parties committing to the covenant. God Himself is the only one Who pledges to, and can keep, a unilateral covenant. He doesn't lay that requirement upon us to make or keep, and aren't we thankful!

Broken bilateral covenants are not mended by the innocent party being forced to continue with their side of the terms, while the breaker, as a repeated lifestyle, violates his vows.

Under certain circumstances, a new covenant or contract may eventually be made between the parties. However, the original is broken. It remains so unless the promise-breaker repents and, with the approval of the injured party, restores and heals the break. A new or renewed contract can be offered that may, or may not, be accepted by the injured party. This is how contract law works.

As Christ's disciples, we must care for those who, despite all their efforts, have had their covenant and their life torn asunder, often viciously, by the unfaithful and in many ways wicked spouse.

Any church can be a target-rich environment for predators for at least the following three reasons.

First, Christian women usually desire to please the Lord and their husbands. It is easy for narcissists to handpick spiritually submissive, but naturally docile, women to satisfy their addictions to control and dominate.

Second, women can be indoctrinated with subtle and overt teachings that truly *godly* women accept the husband's authority without question, elevating his authority in her life above God's.

Third, the abusers recognize their potential to exploit the easy grace without repentance that some denominations extend.

My fervent desire is that the ignorance and the ignoring of domestic abuse, often hidden within the church, can be revealed and recognized. My heartfelt goal is for those in leadership, once enlightened, to be aware of the learning curve ahead of them, for them to commit to learn the nuances of domestic abuse and subsequently answer the call to wield a shepherd's rod and staff to protect Christ's lambs from the wolves in sheep's clothing.

When you read this, I hope you sense a heart of love, warning, and illumination, not rebuke. Thank you so much for investing your time.

Respectfully, your sister in the Lord,
Harriet

C H A P T E R   1

IGNORANCE ENCOUNTERS REALITY

In the 1950s through the 1970s, I was nurtured in a healthy Christian home by parents who celebrated sixty-four years of marriage prior to going home to Jesus in 2017. I have the joy of being married since the early 1980s to my one and only most wonderful husband!

Domestic abuse was quite hidden in decades of the past; it was hushed. Looking back now, I recognize that my younger eyes sometimes saw, but did not comprehend, the damage inflicted upon some spouses.

Our initiation into malignant narcissistic abuse began around 2009, though the cloaked abuse had been ongoing for several decades.

From that introduction point, we have chosen to stand against the menacing manifestation of abuse. Though not our sole encounter with women suffering under domestic abuse, my husband and I walked many years with my sister on the brutal path to her liberation. It is my firm belief that when God teaches any of us through tough times, it is our privilege and responsibility to share what we have learned during those experiences so others may benefit.

Insight has come to me from the trauma surrounding my Sissy's deliverance, as well as the diligent research of the topic, the study of Scripture, and the disclosures of other survivors in my world.

These women were not walking in biblical disobedience. None were petulantly deciding that they just didn't want to be married anymore. Neither had they found someone more attractive. On the contrary, they considered their vows holy before their Lord. Yet they were accused and berated by the abuser as un-submissive or rebellious wives, some for even holding different opinions than the abuser held, regardless of the subject.

The entire existence of abused spouses becomes contaminated by the ugly behavior of their cruel husbands. Males who assault their wives' very humanity dismantle their personhood and destroy their dignity. Most of us wouldn't even speak to, or discipline, our misbehaving dogs with the venom abusers direct to their victims.

Christian women suffering abuse cry out to the Lord to help them be better wives: the kind that they have been conditioned by the abusers' critical lies into believing that they are not. Many have been on their faces before the Lord for years.

Though details differed, most were, or still are, living with an enemy who daily shot them with various emotional projectiles and then jeered at them for having the nerve to emotionally bleed! Many bled due to physical violence.

Have you ever had to lock a room to keep a dangerous person away from you? Have you ever been locked in a room, imprisoned in your own home, by someone you love who is attempting to inflict cruelty upon you? I personally know victims who, at various times, locked themselves in rooms to keep the physical abuser out or have been locked in a room by the abuser to keep them confined and afraid.

Abusers bury their victim's cries with shovels full of contempt. In many cases, the abuser maintains his claim, his image, of being a Christian all the while acting like the devil in the privacy of the home.

In the situation of one woman I know very well, the ultimate goal of the abuser was determined, in retrospect, to have been the eventual suicide of the spouse he preyed upon. In the minds of others, he had planted and cultivated innuendos and made declarations of her supposed mental illness for many years.

Sadly, this tactic is not uncommon, nor is the attempt to involuntarily commit some wives to mental institutions. After years of continual abuse, some spouses are rendered mentally unstable. The real cause of the victim's affliction is only uncovered by those trained to recognize and treat complex post-traumatic stress disorder (c-PTSD).

Many women have children with them in the tomb of abuse. In some of these homes, the children are further victimized by the abuser's physical assaults or sexual exploitation. These mommas watch their children, both younger and adult, contracting diseases of the soul under their father's merciless authority. Some children withdraw into protection mode. Others, tragically, begin to emulate the behaviors of the abuser. These are additional reasons for her to escape, so as to either remove the children from the cancer of abuse or show their adult children a better way.

Thankfully, our church stood with several abused women. It was difficult and unpleasant but expressed the heart of the Father.

Regrettably, some escapees are scorned in ignorant judgment by critics—mainly, and disgracefully, by some people in the church who

- woefully lack the desire to know details *beyond gossip level*;
- are ignorant of the facts;
- display little genuine compassion;
- have even less understanding of the nature of abuse; and
- are inexperienced in rightly dividing (accurately handling, correctly teaching) the Word of Truth.

An abused spouse leaving and filing for divorce does not break the marriage! Sexual fidelity isn't the only part of the covenant two people vow to each other in front of God and witnesses. Fidelity is not always violated by an abuser, but certainly the vows to love, honor, cherish, and provide for are breached by his cruelty and abandonment.

Kicking the abused spouse out of the family home does happen. It is another form of abandonment. The words *desertion* and *abandonment* encompass so much more than the common, but inadequate, definition of simply "him walking out on her." This is explained scripturally quite well in Barbara Roberts' book *Not Under Bondage*.[1]

---

[1] Barbara Roberts, *Not Under Bondage: Biblical Divorce for Abuse, Adultery and Desertion* (Maschil Press, 2008).

Frequently, the male abuser is the one with social and financial power. He is usually the one issuing threats of taking or keeping the children, knowing it will hurt her to be kept apart from her children. This is easily facilitated by our judicial system, which often grants custody to the parent having the best financial ability to support the children.

The abuser can also secretly run up debt in the victim's name during their time living together (it's simple to do) and then default on payment during the separation. Debt that he accrues while they are still legally married is considered to also be her responsibility by creditors, regardless of who made the actual purchases. He can effectively ruin her financially.

It is not unusual for leadership to steer a woman toward legal separation from her abuser, considering separation to be an avenue to save the marriage. In certain States, filing for divorce may be the only protective legal option for an abused woman to retain or regain primary or joint custody or even be granted visitation rights. A legal separation does not afford her those protections, nor does it protect her financial rights. I have walked this road alongside one of my friends.

Good legal counsel is imperative. You may be a spiritual advisor for an abused wife, but without being currently licensed in family law, you are legally and morally ill-equipped to instruct her in this matter. Thus, recommending, or authoritatively commanding, that she simply stay in a condition of separation places you in the undesirable position of overstepping your expertise and spiritual authority.

I would never presume to advise divorce (that's expressly between a woman and her Lord). I will also not debate the subject with those who have only skimmed the surface of divorce in Scripture. Repeated recitation of "God hates divorce," as though it is the only aspect of divorce in God's Word, reveals the necessity of much deeper study beyond traditionally ingrained biases.

Rightly dividing the Word of Truth incorporates the whole counsel of God, the in-depth study of Greek and Hebrew, plus researching the ancient Semitic and Israeli customs. It also means not neglecting the study of scholarly commentaries that explain, especially to us Westerners, what those at the time of the writing of Scripture would have understood culturally.

CHAPTER 2

COME LEARN WITH ME

The Lord gave me specific insight in John 11:39–44 where Jesus calls Lazarus forth from the tomb. Yea! A brother brought back to his grieving sisters! High five! All is well! But the story doesn't end there.

Can you imagine the scene? Mourners and the inquisitive are quietly talking among themselves, "Look! Jesus arrived. What do you think he will He do?" At the call "Lazarus, come forth!" onlookers stand in stunned silence as Lazarus, somehow, exits the place where his shrouded and wrapped body had lain for four days. Anticipating the stench of death, the spectators probably took a step or two backward as Lazarus stumbles, hops, and falls (?!?) through the tomb opening bound like a mummy at a cheesy high school haunted house.

This scene is illustrative of an abused woman fleeing an *already broken marital covenant*. Her head is wrapped in the fog deliberately created for her by the abuser to keep her off balance. She is bound not only by the tactics of abuse leveled at her but also by the c-PTSD brought on by continual long-term trauma.

Appallingly, abusers often cultivate allies with a falsified storyline that portrays the target as bad, unsafe, or mentally ill. This is preventive damage control on his part in case others might believe her claims. His shrewdly constructed web of lies has already undermined her credibility with those who should be her natural defenders. This, too, creates a haze of confusion and pain.

As she emerges, some startled friends and family may recoil at the unmistakable odor of death that trails after her. Certain people withdraw in actual disbelief, especially those desiring to stay within what they imagine are the abuser's good graces. Others, in self-preservation, state their neutrality and abandon her once they observe the abuser pursuing her in anger as she leaves the tomb he carved out for her.

His rage, usually veiled in front of others, now spreads overtly and covertly to anyone who stands with her. This is especially true if he suspects certain individuals might be willing and able to substantiate her testimonies of his undeniably toxic behavior. Intimidation and manipulation are deployed against anyone he suspects might expose his real self.

When attempting to manipulate the target, or others, the self-proclaimed Christian abuser laces his words with Scripture or Christianese. Such an approach is to prop up his self-aggrandized image of spiritual superiority and authority. Our pastors, my husband, and I had this ploy (unsuccessfully) used against us as we stood for true righteousness.

In John 11:35, Jesus wept at the tomb of death. God the Father foreknew that sin would bring death to mankind and warned against it in Genesis 2:17. God did not ordain death. Like original sin brought death, so does current sin. Death brings anguish to the living. Death wasn't supposed to be, and it brings Jesus sorrow.

So it is in marriage where the abuser brings death into a union of oneness that God Himself designed to bring forth life: the two becoming "one." God never designed the bilateral covenant of marriage to be one partner habitually lording manipulation, intimidation, and domination (forced control) over the other. These are evidences of the spirit of witchcraft in operation.[2]

Our loving Father designed human marriage as a type and model of the treasured commitment between Jesus and His cherished Bride, for whom He laid down His life. In Ephesians 5, the apostle Paul teaches that the righteous husband should exhibit the same sacrifice of laying down his life for his wife as Christ has done for the church. God weeps over the cruelty one spouse directs at another. Abuse is sin in any relationship. In marriage, the sin of continual abuse violates the marital covenant, and it brings death.

When abuse is revealed, sometimes, the abuser, or the naive Christian, utters, "Oh, but we are ALL sinners!" Such justification is the abuser's attempt to keep his mask in place and is sin-leveling. The term *sin-leveling* is pretty much self-explanatory: "MY (specific) sin is no worse than YOUR (everyday just because you are human) sin." It is a tactic to silence the opposition.

This technique is utilized to cause the abused person to focus introspectively on their own unrelated sins. Sin-

---

[2] Derek Prince, *Blessing or Curse: You can Choose* (Grand Rapids: Chosen Books, 1990), 66–67.

leveling by the abuser is a diversion employed to draw the spotlight away from his sin and deflect it onto the target and sometimes even onto her advocates. It is a spiritual stronghold that always carries a mental justification for repeated sin.

When "we are all sinners" is uttered by an unthinking believer or family member (to whom the target of abuse has confided in), the insinuation is that she is equally at fault. Perhaps it is said because the person to whom the abuse was divulged is at a loss on how to respond to the target's unexpected disclosure. Nevertheless, it is a pitiless cliché that places the identical weight of responsibility and blame upon the abused as it does upon the offender.

This sin-leveling statement projects as much reproach on an undeserving party as does the equally condemning judgment vocalized as "Well, it takes two!" Are either of these two calloused phrases the attitude a concerned parent would adopt when their child is bullied at school? No, they are not. Domestic abuse is bullying brought into the sanctity of the home.

Sin-leveling by someone other than the abuser shows that the person speaking has serious doubts about the truth or gravity of the abused woman's claims and plight. When sensing the other person's doubts, the target will need to consider if this person is safe for any future discussions of her situation! Her anguished revelation of abuse is distorted into a frivolous "he said, she said" dispute by the person in whom she confided. Consequently, a priceless woman wonders if anyone, including God, will stand up for her.

The realization that this disbelieving person has doubts about the abuse catches her off guard. She may not even consider that she is free to politely refuse to "discuss this deeply personal matter at this time."

If the person acts offended by her decision, she may feel compelled to apologize when she has no need to. Responding with contrition when someone seems offended has been ingrained in her during the years spent attempting to placate the abuser. It takes years for the abused one to lay aside as no longer necessary the automatic reply of "I'm sorry."

Because of the perpetrator's brainwashing, abused Christian women usually have a history of questioning God about what the abuser programmed them into believing is wrong with them. The guilt for "their" troubles in the marriage is squarely placed upon the victim by the abuser. These women pray to be better wives. In their distress, they may justifiably react to the trauma inflicted upon them, but the abuser condemns their responses. To bring down the tension or because the abuser threatens her, the victim may repent of, or apologize for, her understandable reactions. Her reactions may even earn her his criticism that she couldn't be a Christian!

The abuser identifying himself as a Christian denies his claim by his wretched sin against his victim. Submitting one's sin nature to the cleansing blood of Jesus makes us new people. In 2 Corinthians 5:17, Scripture declares that when we authentically receive Jesus as Savior, we are made new in Him. Our nature is changed as we surrender to His sanctification process. We sin. We screw up. We know it. We humbly repent and keep offering ourselves to be transformed into His image, and we are.

Habitual abuse is a different animal altogether!

The abuser repeatedly

- lies to, and about, the human target of his malice;
- toys with the target because it's a game of manipulation—winning is everything;
- steals from her;
- purposely ruins her credit and/or reputation;
- reduces her to poverty;
- attacks her sanity;
- repeats a carefully crafted narrative so others will question her mental stability or character;
- subverts;
- shames;
- ridicules;
- intimidates;
- verbally assaults her personhood;
- threatens her (and sometimes the children);
- sexually abuses her and/or the children (rape, undesired acts, or withholding marital rights);
- rages;
- gaslights;[3]
- restricts access to others, causing isolation;
- physically assaults;
- dispenses "punishment"; and
- murders her.

Abusers control and harm the target by using a mixture of the above behaviors. They always progress in the ways they attack, and they escalate the intensity. Secular

---

[3] "Gaslighting Types, Phases and Phrases," YouTube, https://youtu.be/hN8IMnLdw04.

behavioral specialists acknowledge that abusers only go higher on the abuse scale, never lower. They abuse the target verbally, financially, sexually, psychologically, emotionally, physically, spiritually, relationally, and by restricting access to others.

Worse still, they craft painful parental alienation. They use the children to manipulate the wife, which breaks rapport between mother and child. Sometimes, they exploit the mother/child relationship in other ways to influence legal custody outcomes.

Unquestionably, parental alienation harms the children. Moreover, when the abuser spitefully uses the children to wound her, she then experiences increased distress because of her inability to protect them from him. This rips her heart out.

The abuser escalating to the point of murder is supported by real numbers. The Violence Policy Center reports that of the 1795 females murdered by males in 2019 in the United States, 51 percent (915 victims) were wives, common-law wives, ex-wives, or girlfriends of the offenders. In 2020, the overall number of females murdered by males increased to 2059, which lowered the percentage from the previous year to 47 percent but increased the numbers of intimate partner murders (967 victims).[4]

Abuser escalation is nothing to be taken lightly.

Should the victim come to the end of herself and commit suicide, he can effortlessly explain it away if he has already meticulously built around her the false narrative of

---

[4] "Violence Policy Center, When Men Murder Women," https://vpc.org/studies/wmmw2021.pdf.

mental illness. Then he appears to be the mourning widower, the subject of pity and coveted attention.

All of the above-named behaviors are the repulsive weapons of domination's lifestyle of entitlement. Such a life is completely opposite of the occasional "Oh honey, I was awful to you today, I was wrong. I'm so sorry."

Minimizing abusive behavior under the pretense of having had a bad day cannot be used as an excuse for abusing others. Despite today's soft-on-crime ideology of "It isn't his fault; he had a traumatic childhood" or "He had a poor upbringing," a history of being a target of abuse in one's past does not justify cruelty to others in the present. Earlier experiences undoubtedly influenced, probably even injured, the abuser. But the abuser, like the rest of us, is answerable for chosen brutality in the here and now.

Abusers hide their mistreatment of their target for, at minimum, two reasons. We may not always be able to determine which reason is foremost.

On some level, he knows the abuse is considered wrong by most people, especially in the case of assault and battery. Thus, he abuses in private, away from negative public scrutiny that could lead to legal entanglements.

Also, many abusers are used to rules of life applying to others, but not to themselves. They are the exception. So the individual abuser may believe that such behavior is wrong in the eyes of others, but it is not wrong *for him*. Through deception and his elevated self-image, he has convinced himself that it is his right to treat others abominably.

A *Narcissistic Abuser* is a *BULLY.* He Abuses Because He Can.

We know he is a bully because, like a light switch, an abuser can turn the malevolence off and on *at will* depending upon who is present to observe (and expose) his actions. This can't be emphasized enough: when anyone can control their behavior depending upon the audience, their behavior is a *choice*.

Habitual-consistent-chronic-lifestyle-practice—these words completely differentiate between abuse and the occasional jerk behavior that plagues us all. For example, those who practice medicine earned their title of doctor. Those who practice abuse are abusers. They have earned that label. Being good at covert abusing feeds their ego like an illicit drug. Covert abuse is his drug of choice. Successful hidden abuse gives the wrongdoer what he craves, while it shields him from exposure and potential legal retribution.

The practiced narcissistic abuser is an actor in his own play. He wrote the script specifically for his character, and he is really good at creating illusion. He draws in his audience using the measured delivery of his lines, his costumes, and masks. Having refined his craft, he knows all the techniques and emotional seduction that entice the audience, unaware, into his performance.

"Audience," not friends—those who believe they are friends are props and spectators that he can use as allies against his scapegoat (target of abuse). When their usefulness is complete, they are discarded. Those who have managed to go behind the curtain of deception and observe him without makeup, and a mask that is slipping, are the first to be rejected. There truly is a phantom in this opera, and nothing he does is for anyone's benefit but his own.

Does every abuser utilize this skill? No. But those who do execute it well and fool many an onlooker.

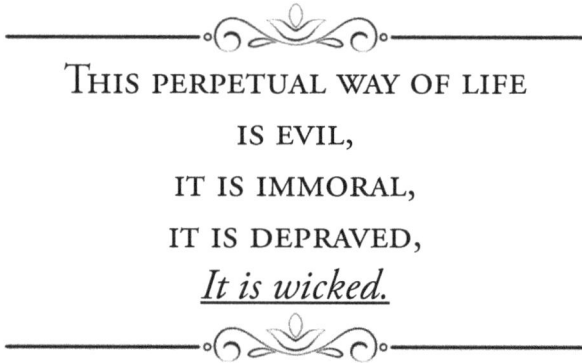

THIS PERPETUAL WAY OF LIFE

IS EVIL,

IT IS IMMORAL,

IT IS DEPRAVED,

It is wicked.

An abused woman is living in a tomb surrounded by death. She has been repeatedly and purposely wounded, while her essence, her personhood, decays. Abuse assaults her dignity and her humanity. She has no say, no power; she is slowly erased as though she was never there. Self-worth? It's gone.

The abuser's choice to torment the woman he vowed to love is the stone he rolled in front of the tomb she suffers in. When something raises her awareness that she is actually the victim of abuse, a newly awakened perception causes that stone to be dislodged.

Even if it's just a little movement of the stone, the fresh air of revelation begins rushing in. Her understanding of the situation begins to be adjusted—she realizes that she isn't the problem after all! Progressive death has been imposed upon her. She is infected with it through the selfish choices of another, and so are their children.

The wedding vows promising to love, cherish, provide for, and maintain fidelity give a glimpse into the marriage every bride is longing for and has every right to expect. Heartbroken, many discover that their fiancé wore an impenetrable façade of calculated goodness, yes, even godliness. He excelled at displaying his fake self to fool everyone, especially his bride. That disguise is conveniently discarded in private once the vows are spoken. A union joyfully anticipated by one spouse is thus made a sham by oaths professed by the other under false pretenses.

When she seeks help through the church or court systems, she frequently finds polluted fingers of family, friends, church members, or leadership pointed at her. Ignorant and/or arrogant accusations that she "broke the marriage" are a knife in her heart that is so weary from trying to make it work. The abuser's unrepentant, continual ruthlessness volleyed against her broke the vows, and thus the marriage, before she ever crawled out of the tomb!

Unfortunately, there are some who see this woman staggering out who tell her she must return to the tomb of death. They insist she has no right to be rescued from the destruction, decay, and death because, after all, *she* chose to marry this man!

No, she married *the man he pretended to be.* Only those with hardened hearts cannot, or will not, comprehend the previous sentence. Even in modern times, contracts and covenants are held as void when signed as an act of *fraud* and especially when the terms are violated.

This verdict of shame, and the insistence that she stay in the tomb regardless of abuse, *makes "marriage" the idol to be worshiped.* Read that again.

The abuser's propaganda, and his planned narrative of her supposed shortcomings spoken to others, often lays the foundation for others to judge her prematurely and in error.

Bystanders, with no authority over the target, but possessing biased or sanctimonious perceptions, deem this marriage to be deteriorating because of something the victim has done. SHE is guilty; SHE is disrespectfully casting dispersions on her husband publicly; SHE is a failure; SHE is overreacting; SHE made a bad choice; SHE must have been out of God's will! SHE isn't trying hard enough, praying the right way, or enduring long enough. (Who decides how long is *enough?*)

CLEARLY STATED:
CIVIL DIVORCE IS THE
LEGAL DOCUMENTATION
THAT RATIFIES THE DECISION
THE ABUSER MADE TO
BREAK COVENANT,
TO BREAK VOWS...
TO BREAK THE MARRIAGE.

Divorcing a mate because of, for example, falling out of love or desiring a different mate is defined as a treacherous divorce. It is not sanctioned in any way.

When a husband's abuse ruptures the marriage, and she finds it necessary to authenticate that breach through legal divorce proceedings, critics open their Bibles to Mark 10:9. Accusations arise that she violated that command by putting asunder what God joined. The accusers can't seem to make the connection that the hard-hearted abuser already tore asunder what God had joined; she is only legalizing the broken status he created.

If Mark 10:9 has been violated by the abuser, we must not make Mark 10:12 applicable to the innocent victim.

She is not nonchalantly putting away her husband just so she is free to move on to greener pastures. On the contrary, a truly abused wife is justifiably requesting, as her legal remedy, the Bill of Divorcement noted in Deuteronomy 24:1–2.

If the husband is abusing her as a lifestyle, with no confession or fruits of repentance, it is quite obvious to anyone with a beating heart that she has "found no favor" in his merciless eyes.

In such cases, the church should not require that she remain a hostage to a malevolent spouse slowly killing all parts of her personhood. In fact, in 1 Corinthians 5:11, Paul considers the person matching the description of the abusing husband to *not* be a brother in the Lord.

Unfortunately, those unfairly judging the woman escaping her husband's abuse subsequently treat her as if the couple's bilateral marriage covenant was a *unilateral* covenant that only she must live up to. Their condemnation is erroneous.

In a bilateral covenant, if either party breaches the terms, the covenant is broken.

Only GOD can declare and maintain the aforementioned unilateral covenant. He demonstrated this ability with Noah, the animals, and the very earth and again with Abraham. We need to stop insisting that the abuse target bears a unilateral (sole) responsibility for keeping the marriage together!

The irrationality of holding her accountable for the abuser's actions is akin to attributing a rape victim's location, dress, or smile for a friend or stranger's choice to perpetrate sexual violence (also despicable).

An abused wife is not perfect and may be responsible before the Lord for other aspects of marital issues or her own inward attitudes and trespasses. She is not responsible for the decision on the part of her spouse to sin against her by breaking the promises made on their wedding day.

As we review John 11:1–44, we find no indication that Jesus's friend Lazarus did something particularly sinful that permitted illness unto death, as the Pharisees taught. Was his death solely a result of living in a world cursed through Adam's original sin? Scripture doesn't tell us. Jesus apparently didn't care what caused it. He simply raised Lazarus to life again— *because that's what Jesus does. He brings life out of death and sets the captives free*, and He glorifies the Father in the process.

If there is detailed exegesis on verse 44, I haven't yet heard it in six decades of sermons.

> Jesus said to them, "Loose him, and let him go."

Do you see it? Lazarus needed help removing the burial garments wound around him *because he did not bind himself!* Thus, Jesus commanded the witnesses to release Lazarus from his bindings.

Amid joy at renewed life, there were practical needs to be addressed. As the bindings came off, Lazarus was naked in front of everyone! Moles, scars, and every private part lay open to be viewed by those who loved him and by those who were merely there out of curiosity. Lazarus needed clothing to cover his nakedness.

His financial affairs, having been rearranged as a consequence of his death, had to be reordered to care for him in his remaining years. Four days dead with no food? He could have been famished for a good home-cooked meal and a drink of water.

Jesus calls the abused wife out of the tomb. Observers are stunned and skeptical:

> "Are you sure he abused you? We have never seen that side of him!"
>> Do they expect him to be abusive in front of witnesses?

> "But he didn't hit you, right?"
>> Physical brutality is only one of MANY ways to abuse someone!

> "What did you do to instigate his actions?"
>> Ah, yes. Tit for tat. Spoken to an admittedly imperfect woman but one who has done everything humanly possible to placate him and elude his abuse.

> "But he is a <deacon, pastor, missionary, godly man, doctor, fill in the blank>; he couldn't be like you are painting him!"
>> I have no words for this level of naiveté.

> "Just trust the Lord; God can fix anything."
>> In other words, keep enduring evil. While God often creates opportunities for a wicked person to come to Him and change, He doesn't override the will of man. An abuser is nothing

if not willful and right in his sight. Because he feels there is no need for God to "fix" him, there is no desire to change, nor any sincere effort.

"If your allegations are true, why didn't you say something before now?"

As confirmed by this question, she correctly expected that people would not believe her.

Her abuser commanded her to not air *their* dirty laundry; doing so would expose him.

If she speaks out, he will rebuke her as rebellious and disobedient. She knows from experience to expect to be punished in some manner for her noncompliance to his commands.

The above remarks are all examples of inherent disbelief, even when uttered with a tone of concern. Such comments reveal the inquirer's ignorance of the deliberately concealed nature of abuse and the resistance of the abuser to repentance.

Those who have never lived in the tomb of abuse are oblivious of the shame, the threats, and the paralyzing fear a woman must overcome *just to admit* she's being abused, even to herself! Without recognizing the effect of their questions upon the target, they add insult to injury even if they truly care about her.

"Did you pray about this?"

What kind of STUPID asks that of a known Christ follower? She's been weeping before the Lord, sometimes for decades. For a devoted Christian, this question is insulting and degrading. It is dreadfully condescending. In so many words, it implies that the abused woman isn't as intelligent, or as spiritual, as the inquirer.

Asking how to be agreeing in prayer with a woman who has just disclosed abuse would be the wiser and more compassionate question to ask. An offer to agree in prayer raises the subject of consulting the Lord for decisions but with kindness! Sensitive wording will not convey the offensive presumption that she is perhaps prayer-less and somehow less than in any way. Her abuser has already condemned her as never enough; she doesn't need it subtly implied by anyone else.

As Lazarus had practical needs, so does the woman leaving abuse. Because He is in the business of releasing the captives, we are His hands. Jesus commands us to remove the death bindings *the abuser* wrapped around her.

The abuse survivor, like Lazarus, is naked. Exposed is the raw agony of broken promises, shattered dreams, rejection, perhaps loss of financial security, and physical infirmity either from the abuser's hands or the stress his treatment of her creates. Her confidence is ruined by schemes of mental and emotional torment, shame, abandonment, poverty, threats, and FEAR! She needs protective covering that goes beyond mere clothing, which she may also desperately need.

The woman coming out of an abusive marriage needs to be gently washed and redressed, sometimes again and again, with kindness, compassion, and the Word of God. She has, unquestionably, been indoctrinated by the abuser's words and actions that pronounce her hopelessly unlovable and valueless. Therefore, she must be patiently filled with the assurance of her heavenly Father's limitless and passionate love for her.

Trusting again can be a fearful thing to one whose trust has been intentionally, progressively annihilated. Her abuser distorts her reality on a regular basis. Disorientation in the world outside the marriage battleground is the rule, not the exception. Consequently, her frame of reference for normal versus abnormal is fragmented.

Though her abuser might try to convince people otherwise, talking in halting speech is not a mental deficiency. It is an outcome of protecting herself. She's been forced to play a psychotic game where the abuser changes the unwritten rules with no warning. She's afraid to say something that enrages him or that he will twist and use against her later. She must review everything she is trying to say while the words are forming on her lips.

As she is speaking, changes of his facial expressions tell her that she must instantly search for a safer word than the one she planned on, and consequently, she stumbles on her own tongue. He mocks her verbal blunders. When she voices something today that was okay yesterday, he switches what is acceptable to keep her off balance. Her need to suddenly adapt to his inconsistencies keeps her questioning her words. His frightening unpredictability strengthens his control over her.

Often she is penniless. Starting over is nearly impossible because of his premeditated manipulation and abuse of finances. Whether not allowed or forced to work outside the home, many wives are required to ask for cash and then required to account for every penny of their expenditures. The joint checkbook might be off limits. She might be given the debit card, but no pin, so any purchase is run through as a credit he can monitor.

Her purchases are probed and criticized. It is not unusual that the offending spouse spends money extravagantly while disapprovingly scrutinizing her rather small household expenditures. Joint accounts that she is refused access to often have monetary transfers into his individual account or are suddenly brought to zero. Money she is rightly entitled to is placed out of her reach.

The Bible has many passages revealing how God feels about abusers, oppressors, and their victims.

> The Spirit of the LORD GOD is upon Me,
> because the LORD has anointed Me to
> preach good tidings to the poor;
> He has sent Me to heal
> the brokenhearted,
> to proclaim liberty to the captives,
> and the opening of the prison
> to those who are bound.
> —Isaiah 61:1 NKJV

> The Spirit of the LORD is upon Me,
> because He has anointed Me to
> preach the gospel to the poor;

He has sent Me to heal
the brokenhearted,
to proclaim liberty to the captives
and recovery of sight to the blind,
to set at liberty those who are oppressed.
—Luke 4:18 NKJV

Some command our part to play:

How long will you judge unjustly
and show partiality to the wicked? Selah.
Vindicate the weak and fatherless;
do justice to the afflicted and destitute.
rescue the weak and needy;
deliver them out of the
hand of the wicked.
—Psalm 82:2–4 NASB95

Thus says the LORD, "Do
justice and righteousness,
and deliver the one who has been
robbed from the power of his oppressor."
—Jeremiah 22:3a NASB95

He who oppresses the poor
reproaches his Maker,
but he who honors Him has
mercy on the needy.
—Proverbs 14:31 NKJV

Open your mouth for the mute,
for the rights of all the unfortunate.
Open your mouth, judge righteously,
and defend the rights of the
afflicted and needy.
—Proverbs 31:8, 9 NASB95

Learn to do good; seek justice,
rebuke the oppressor;
defend the fatherless, plead
for the widow.
—Isaiah 1:17 NKJV

The character of God the Father is displayed in the preceding verses. Weigh them carefully. As you ruminate on the above verses, ask yourself these questions:

- Is a man who basically enslaves his wife keeping the holy covenant of matrimony he agreed to?
- Does "I do" biblically disqualify an abused woman from being rescued and her basic human rights upheld?
- Does the ring on the finger of an abused woman revoke the biblical mandate to defend such an afflicted and powerless person from the wicked oppressor?
- Does biblical mercy and justice only apply to the unmarried woman?

Again, I do not promote or advise divorce, but then neither did Jesus! He spoke to men, not to women, about divorce being allowed only because of the hardness of the men's hearts. In the days of Jesus and up until today, men are generally the power brokers, the more financially secure, and endowed with greater physical strength. A man can more easily subjugate and control a woman.

There is nothing that demonstrates the hardness of a man's heart toward God more than the abuse of the woman he vowed to cherish or their children. When the bilateral marriage covenant is broken by the sinful actions of a hardened, unrepentant, reprobate heart, we must carefully examine scripture with the character of God as our light of interpretation, and we must not step into the role God reserves for Himself when a woman is prayerfully examining the options for saving her emotional or physical life or that of her children.

CHAPTER 3

ESPECIALLY FOR PASTORS

In my adult life, I have heard two of my pastors (thank you, Rob and Mike) make this declaration from the pulpit: "If I find out you are abusing your wife I *will* get your butt thrown in jail!" (Yes, just that descriptive.) I was so proud of these men who publicly announced that they wouldn't knowingly stand for such degrading and criminal behavior.

The ultimate tragedy is not the
oppression and cruelty by the
bad people, but the silence over
that by the good people.
Dr. Martin Luther King Jr.

Regrettably, stories abound from women suffering relentless abuse who are appallingly oppressed by their own pastors. Their pastors and churches disgracefully turned on them, even to the point of dis-fellowship, when the women recognized the vows to them had been broken in such a way that escape was necessary.

It is my understanding that most seminaries and Bible colleges do not teach how to recognize, or handle cases of domestic abuse in the church. If they do, it is not a course that covers the depth that is necessary in such devastating circumstances. I would be grateful to be informed of any Christian schools of higher learning that have any comprehensive course that teaches the fundamentals of abuse. There seems to be no training on how to identify abuse, the tactics and deception involved, the effect on or care for the victim, or the legal concerns the victim and the church may encounter.

The church at large, to our shame, is profoundly lagging behind the secular world in identifying and fighting against abuse or even rescuing the woman escaping her abuser. Brothers and sisters, that ought not to be! Shepherds need to be taught how to recognize the snake of abuse, courageously defy it, and be prayerfully anointed for the battle. Breakout sessions at annual denominational conventions would be an excellent start!

I cannot exhort you strongly enough to pursue education from the many resources available regarding abuse, signs of victimization, tactics used, and the various deceptions the perpetrator employs.

Even more important is that YOU do not assume that the abuser is a Christ-follower just because he attends your church. Abusing anyone contradicts the new life in Christ that is imparted to those who are truly saved. Respectfully, do not presuppose that you are qualified to spiritually, or in any other way, "fix" him just because you have Reverend in front of your name. No offense intended—just fact.

Anytime you as a pastor are across the desk from a broken wife exposing her abuse-injured soul, your subsequent private time is of supreme importance. I suggest falling before the Lord in humility and submission, admitting that in your own self you are inadequate, inexperienced, and profoundly human.

In that position of surrender, a priority prayer is for protection from the spirit of deception that will most certainly seek to cloud your vision. Stay with the Lord until He empowers you with the discernment of spirits and gives you direction for each particular case you encounter.

Without Holy Spirit insight, plus training in dealing with narcissistic abuse, most pastors are in over their heads. This is especially true if they grew up in the incubator of the church and attended higher Christian education.

The narcissist keenly recognizes spiritual inexperience, worldly naiveté, and gullibility. He *counts* on it! But even if you've not yet encountered such evil, there is no excuse not to learn now. It is reasonable to assume that, in your future, you will be confronted with the need to protect the lambs God has entrusted into your care. It is wisdom to gather knowledge now.

Once the abused finally breaks her silence and begs for help, churches, too often, force joint "marriage" counseling. In all seriousness, this is the most dangerous requirement you can place upon the victim! You are compelling the woman into a position of close quarters with her spouse while he manipulates the counselors and the narrative. Bluntly, you are an accessory to any revictimization she experiences.

Abuse is NOT Marital incompatibility; it is NOT a communication problem. It is a demonstration of egregious sin and, often, criminality.

If the wife has fearfully disclosed abuse to you, she has just carried out *the bravest thing she has ever done*. At no time should she and the reported abuser (even if yet unconfirmed) be counseled in the same room! Each party must be interviewed separately as you seek the Lord for discernment. It's a no-brainer; nevertheless, countless survivors have related horror stories of pastors forcing them into joint counseling with their abuser.

In an abusive marriage, it is common for the abuser to coach his target as to what she is allowed to say, whether it is something as simple as a church fellowship or as serious as joint counseling sessions. Disobedience to his coaching, plus exposing him and his tormenting actions, will lead to various types of punishment later.

Punishment is meted out as if to a disobedient child or rebellious slave. It can be as understated as the "silent treatment" or loud raging in anger. Some churches even support a humiliating spanking. Violent physical assault that requires medical intervention is not uncommon.

In any venue, but especially counseling, the target may look to the abuser to see if he approves of her answering the question that was directed to her. Did you catch that look during the meet-and-greet time at church?

Alternately, he may simply answer on her behalf as though she is incapable of answering for herself. I've witnessed this on a Sunday morning, and I'm not a pastor.

The abuser may also insist that this is just her problem and that *she* needs marriage counseling to be a good wife.

If he is a malignant narcissistic abuser, he will enjoy calmly toying with the counselor to see how much of his meticulously scripted plot the counselor or pastor will believe. Regrettably, many pastors will have little to no idea they are being duped.

> Well-crafted damage control
> is not repentance.
> It takes discernment to
> know the difference.
>
> Pastor Garris Elkins

An abusing spouse may brag of the ways he is trying to make the relationship work, but contend that she is not. He may state that he is the good Christian, but she is not. The victim may try to protest, but by this time, she has usually learned her lesson, so to speak, and retreats into muteness. These are wildly waving red flags! If he is praising his own efforts like a blowhard, even in calm tones, but condemning her while she sits silent and subdued, you are almost certainly peering into the tomb of abuse.

When an abuser's behaviors are pointed out to him as wrong, there will usually be no guilt or shame admitted to. As stated previously, even if others view his abuse as immoral or sinful, the rules are for others, not for him.

Perhaps you hear from his lips the accusation, unsupported by any facts, that she is this or that, such as an alcoholic, a child abuser, a homosexual, or an adulteress. Consider that such accusations are sometimes an additional method used by narcissistic abusers. Called projection, this approach "projects" onto her the behaviors he is already guilty of but is desperately concealing. Subsequently, he attempts to establish her as the individual to be questioned as the wrongdoer.

Employing fake victimhood is the attempt to divert the focus away from his abuse and onto the target or onto those that perhaps removed him from a favored role or position. Like a magician's sleight of hand, presenting himself as the injured party is his endeavor to point your attention anywhere other than his own conduct.

As noted throughout this book, a joint marriage counseling session, after abuse has been reported, is irresponsible. The counseling pastor should assume that he or she will not receive accurate information from the abuser. Furthermore, he should anticipate incomplete communication from the frightened target. It bears repeating, when abuse is alleged, joint marital counseling should always be considered as extremely hazardous to the target and will only reveal information of uncertain quantity and quality.

The solitary redeeming attribute of the *error* of joint counseling is the potential to reveal abusive clues to a pastor or counselor who already suspects as much and is trained in recognizing abuse tactics and the responses of the victim.

If engaged in a preliminary joint session, solely to ascertain future counseling options or because the abuser hauled her in, keep one ear open to a braggart coolly reciting the faults of the spouse as you keep both eyes on the target. This awareness is helpful even in an individual session. Watch her closely. Shame and fear emanate from her. While listening to what she says, study how she says it: her posture, body language, speech, and eyes. He might be confident in his sessions; he is "Teflon®"—accusations never stick to him—but she is *prey*, and she knows it. You need to figure it out quickly!

Male pastors, if your wife is a perceptive woman of God, consider bringing her into all the sessions when determining what type of counseling is appropriate: private or, God forbid, joint. Her presence might provide female comfort. Her God-given intuition will probably pick up additional insight you need.

Especially in today's world, if you are a male pastor, it is wisdom to have your wife or other female staff member in the room when counseling any woman. If you are a female pastor, use your discretion regarding having another woman present when counseling a woman.

I personally would not advise a female of any title counseling the accused male abuser, especially alone. He already "lords" his maleness over one woman. Exercising his perceived male superiority, not to mention his subtle manipulative abilities, over another woman would encourage his power trip even more.

No matter your gender, if you have your prayer language, use it privately before any counseling session. You need discernment from the Holy Spirit!

Psychopath? Sociopath? Big, dumb, ham-handed alcoholic? All three are dangerous and hard to distinguish between, sometimes even for professionals. A pastor misdiagnosing an abusive situation as merely a problematic marital relationship can cause grave consequences for the abused person. And I use the word *grave* intentionally.

True Christians do not generally purpose to do horrendous things to one another. We submit to the Holy Spirit so we are changed into the likeness of Jesus. As a result, we don't often imagine wicked people, especially those claiming a walk with Christ, doing loathsome things, until we encounter it firsthand and are stunned.

May I suggest that you never, ever, underestimate the depths of evil that an abuser is capable of. This especially holds true regarding a habitually narcissistic abuser feigning Christianity. They have already allowed demonic influence to rule in their lives. And demons know no bottom. These types of abusers only care about not getting exposed or caught.

As a pastor encountering domestic abuse, you are dealing with at least the spirit of witchcraft and, no doubt, the Jezebel spirit. Deception, outright lies, control, and manipulation are favored tools; be in prayer to know which entity you are encountering and how the Lord would have you proceed.

From a godly perspective, if a man is truly walking with the Lord (which includes honoring his vows to the wife of his covenant), she will not be coming to you in fear!

The health or disease in a marriage, over time, will undoubtedly be reflected in the wife's normal, everyday face. In a devout Christian marriage, the husband (as well as wife), walking in the light of God's love and in submission to his Lord's authority, will have a demonstratively penitent, growing-more-like-Jesus's heart. He sorrows over the times he misses the mark. Placing her needs above his own is visible affirmation of his walk, and growth, in the Lord. I know—I am married to that man!

Once more, narcissistic abusers believe they are never wrong, so there is nothing of which to repent, just to conceal. They are gods in their own estimation. They may pretend penitence for a little while, to project an image of cooperation, but they generally cannot sustain make-believe change for long.

Words are not sufficient evidence that an abuser truly wants a healthy, God-honoring, marriage.

"I don't want a divorce" can mean
- I don't want the exposure;
- I don't want the expense; and
- I don't want my reputation sullied.

"I want to save my marriage" can mean
- I still need her subservience;
- The prop of a wedding ring is still useful to me; and

- The use of we, our, and us pronouns is advantageous to my position.

"I want to work on my marriage" can mean

- I want you to correct her thinking so she stops complaining;
- I want you to tell her to submit to me; and
- I want others to believe I want the marriage to work.

Are any of the above statements apologies, repentance, or confessions to the wife of the wrongs he committed against her? No. If words of remorse or apology are uttered, great! Write them down, and date them. Wait for fruit to appear and mature. Reconciliation or restoration should never be the immediate plan after hearing those words. The target's safety comes first.

> Behavior modification without heart
> transformation is akin to ripping all
> the apples off the apple tree, stapling
> bananas in their place, and then
> trying to convince others of how
> amazing this new banana tree is. That
> is exactly what abusers are willing
> to do if they think we'll buy it.
> Rev. Chris Moles[5]

---

[5] Chris Moles's behavior modification quote, http://www.chrismoles.org/news/2016/2/26/qge7lrg1rilltduckzyyxvya6y8zsz.

No one changes unless, and until, they want to humbly submit to biblical change beginning with confession, followed by repentance and restitution. This will necessitate abundant learning and accountability.

Confession is not an apology, though it might and should include an apology. It positively is not "I'm sorry you feel that way." Confession is admittance of wrongdoing without excuses.

Repentance is not feeling sorry for one's actions, though a truly repentant person should feel sorrow over their sins. Repentance is to turn away from what one was doing that caused the pain, to change one's behavior.

Restitution accepts responsibility for, if possible, repaying the debt, the injury, or the consequences of the sinful behavior.

Can the targeted spouse affirm that she has heard a confession of his wrongs (to her face), seen the fruits of repentance, and (if applicable) received gracious and generous restitution? If not, you are well on your way of determining the genuineness of the abuser's claims to being a changed man.

A truly repentant man will recognize and graciously accept the fact that the more delicate vessel, his wife, must be safe from him. An honestly repentant heart will desire to see her rest in the safety of his kindness. He will want to repair damages, be they physical, emotional, or financial. Sincere repentance and humility are key. In such rare cases of sincerity, I highly recommend Restoration Ministries.[6]

---

[6] Ed Glaspey, "Rebuilding the Foundation of Life," Restoration Ministries, Junction City, Oregon. There are classes on-campus, offered at churches, and online, for healing from life's wounds and sin: https://restoration.net/

Phony repentance is a frequently employed manipulative tool. Time must be invested to ascertain if fruits of repentance are visible, growing, and, most critical, *lasting*. Burn this phrase into your mental archive: Only believe behavior—consistent, long-term behavior.

Though it is acknowledged in mental health circles that a narcissistic abuser could change with enough strong desire and dedication to do so, they also admit it is highly unlikely. Behavioral change just to keep the relationship can be merely an appeasement maneuver. However, Jesus can change a heart that is willing to admit sin, repent, and grow.

Weigh over time the behavior of any abuser that suddenly expresses having a "come to Jesus" moment. Again, only believe long-term behavior. Think marathon, not sprint. Relating such an experience can often be part of an underhanded strategy known as hoovering[7] to suck her back in so she can feed his narcissistic needs (aka narcissistic supply).

A Christian woman who has invested so much time, prayer, and emotion into keeping the marriage together might not recognize the dishonesty of hoovering the first time he employs it against her. Too many women have even remarried the same man, much to their later regret, after this deception was successfully deployed against them.

---

testimonies/. *The author knows and loves* many of the staff members of Restoration Ministries and has gone through the Restoration course on campus. I have seen the fruit of healing and highly recommend the course! Pastors: Consider hosting Restoration Ministries at your church. Most people are wounded in ways we aren't privy to.

7   "Hoovering," https://lonerwolf.com/hoovering.

This hoovering maneuver might also escape the notice of a pastor desiring to keep the marriage together but failing to adequately identify and deal strongly with the vows already broken by the abuser. Be watchful for such devices! Be attentive against your own subconscious desire to "save the marriage at all costs." You aren't the one paying the cost.

"After all I've done to change!"

"I've done 'X' like she asked; when is it ever going to be enough?"

"I said I was sorry; how many more times do I have to say it?"

Is the abuser making similar remarks in an irritated or exasperated voice? Do statements like these signify a broken and contrite heart? Expressions similar to these commonly mean he is concentrating on impressing others with his outward acts, instead of focusing on the inward spiritual development of his character, along with growing into being a safe person.

This kind of impatient frustration can be an indication of an abuser following the *letter* of the law just enough to appear to be cooperating, yet not really transforming.

Following the *spirit* of the law will require laying down his life to humbly and sincerely confess his sinful behavior to his wife. Following that, he must learn to walk with Jesus with integrity and heal the heart he broke. Should the victim see enough fruits of repentance to desire to reconcile with him, there should be visible growth into him being her *lover*, not her *master*.

Perseverance and repentant surrender to godly marital health is the attitude we should be watching for. Such an attitude could look like confessing that he was deplorable to her, that he is at fault for his behavior, and that he will do anything for however long it takes to heal her and deserve her love.

In her struggles to trust him again, we should also see him display gentle, humble patience.

The pastor that married us found himself corrected by the Holy Spirit and taught his congregation this profound concept:

> I need to love my wife the way she
> needs to be loved; not the way I
> think she should be satisfied with.
>
> Pastor Rob Tucker

Lengthy, **supervised accountability** is absolutely necessary to confirm **righteous, permanent change**. It is not a quick fix. Even a heart truly committed to now honor his wife and change his behavior requires resolute effort. His heart must sincerely be submitted to Jesus, renouncing former ungodly habits and thought patterns and then replacing them with righteous conduct and mindset.

Is there a sincere attitude of brokenness over wounding this woman he promised to love and care for? Are you seeing true sorrow and humility or self-defense and excuses?

Often, the victim is preached at by leadership and others about her need to forgive the abuser. Yes, of course, but forgiveness is between the injured party and God. It never has to be face to face with her abuser! Forgiveness is not extracting revenge but giving the offenses up to the Lord and letting Him deal with the offender. The forgiveness muscle usually must be exercised repeatedly as abusers are fond of poking the wound they created. Forgiveness also does not mean that everything past and current is okay now.

Reconciliation requires trust. Trust to reconcile only comes with true repentance evidenced by fruit—fruit exhibited over extended periods of accountability. People advising reconciliation just because the victim forgave the perpetrator are ignorant of the definition of the two concepts.

I hate snakes. I can forgive one if it bit me, but I could never reconcile with one. The only trust that exists between us is that I trust it to bite me the first chance it gets. Therefore, I stay away from snakes. I will also avoid any person who attempts to make me reconcile with a snake. Knowing my aversion and distrust of them, that person would not have my best interests at heart.

The analogy can equally be applied to an abused wife and especially anyone trying to convince her to live again with her snake. Nowhere in God's Word have I found instructions to reconcile with evildoers!

Please understand that if the separated abused wife chooses to not reconcile with her abuser, it in no way means she has not forgiven him. Forgiveness and reconciliation are totally different, and things that are different are not the same.

Reconciliation is not advised until, and unless, the *victimized spouse* makes the determination that a good history of the fruits of repentance is in evidence, not just an apple here or there, and that is a judgment call only she can make.

The narcissistic abuser is skilled in deception, deflection, and reading authority figures that he is attempting to manipulate (you). Locate licensed PROFESSIONAL abuse counselors in your area and keep a list—it might come in handy. Have at your fingertips resources in your area for women fleeing domestic violence. If you are at a loss for those services, ask your local law enforcement agency for recommendations.

> The heart is deceitful above all things,
> and desperately wicked; who can know it?
> —Jeremiah 17:9 NKJV

The idea that every abusive person, especially those that self-identify as Christian, always and inherently possesses some good in them and can be turned from their dark side is false. Release that misguided belief! It is a fairy tale from the movies.

Turning from the darkness of their choice to abuse others is only possible if and when they choose to repent before the Lord and become teachable. We cannot cajole their deceived minds to exchange their wickedness for some supposed goodness buried inside them. Abuse isn't a misunderstanding of how to treat people. It is an issue of a selfish heart and grievous sin.

Demons, using the mind, heart, and will of a cooperative subject, can be very subtle in their schemes. The strategies utilized through and by the abuser are always self-centered, wicked, and full of ulterior motives. Be wary. Be informed.

Have coffee with a few police officers and, if they are willing to dredge up repugnant memories, allow them to paint a picture for you of the outcomes of wickedness that sheltered Christians seldom see.

Arrange lunch (and foot the bill) with an ER nurse or doctor working at a hospital in the gritty underside of the city. Tell them you want to learn about abuse so you can help others, and then listen.

Make appointments to interview leaders of local safe houses for women escaping abuse. Their office and safe house addresses are wisely undisclosed, no doubt even to you. Offer to meet them at a public location. Treat them to lunch. Ask questions. Be open for suggestions. Inquire as to what ways your church can partner with them to help! Learn what the experienced have seen.

> To the pure, all things are pure; but to
> those who are defiled and unbelieving,
> nothing is pure, but both their mind
> and their conscience are defiled.
> They profess to know God, but by
> their deeds they deny Him, being
> detestable and disobedient and worthless
> (reprobate) for any good deed.
> —Titus 1:15,16 NASB95

An abuser who defrauds the wife of his sacred promise, in any manner, will almost certainly have no reluctance cheating State social services and/or the State and Federal governments. The IRS can provide copies of *jointly* filed returns, for her to review for accuracy, if she has no access to the originals. If tax documents expose fraudulent declarations or her signature as forged, she can request the IRS to provide her an innocent spouse document (form 8857). If she knows she is eligible for part of a tax refund, there is an injured spouse document (form 8379). Tax advice is undoubtedly necessary. The abused wife may not know this unless you inform her. This is especially vital if her abuser has excluded her from all of their family finances. Please share this important information!

Perhaps your denomination does not support your endeavors to help those dying under domestic abuse. Consider contacting other pastors in your area to ask for ideas. Be aware of churches that demand adherence to strict patriarchy or hyper-complementarianism.[8] Their doctrines will generally sacrifice the victimized spouse on the altars of male supremacy and marriage permanence. Grace and mercy for the target of evil abuse are uncommon.

Forcing one spouse to stay, and be martyred by the other spouse, to save the marriage *makes marriage the idol* to be served. While we never want to see a so-called treacherous divorce based on mere preferences, there is still only one unforgivable sin, and it isn't divorce. Divorce because of purposely implemented abuse is not based on preference.

While divorce, or the abuse that might necessitate it, was never God's design, we can testify that God's Word

---

[8] "Hyper-complementarianism and Domestic Abuse," https://kylejhoward.com/counseling-articles/hyper-complementarianism-domestic-abuse.

absolutely teaches against the sin of idolatry and certainly against the sin of oppressing others.

The apostle Paul, in Romans 1:28–32, identifies the traits of reprobates. Refresh your memory of that passage. It might be wise to keep a list of those characteristics in your drawer to refer to when considering the attributes of a suspected abuser.

Depending upon how far they have fallen, you will find many to almost every one of Paul's descriptive adjectives displayed in the life of the overt and covert abuser.

Additionally, in 1 Corinthians 5:9–13, the apostle Paul is teaching the Corinthians about not associating with those claiming to be Christians but are practicing a life of sin. Among the several descriptors of sinful behavior, Paul included *railer* (aka reviler). According to Strong's *Exhaustive Concordance of the Bible*[9], *railer* means "abusive, blackguard, reviler."

Paul also adds *extortioner* (aka swindler in NASB). Strong's concordance amplifies *extortioner*[10] to include "robber" and "ravening," which according to the *Collins Dictionary*,[11] is defined as "greedily searching for prey" and "predatory behavior."

An abuser falsely identifying as a Christian will have a mixture of verse 11's behaviors active in their life and in their treatment of the abuse target.

---

[9] Blue Letter Bible, "Strong's G3060—loidoros," https://www.blueletterbible.org/lexicon/g3060/kjv/tr/0-1/.

[10] Blue Letter Bible, "Strong's G727—arpax," https://www.blueletterbible.org/lexicon/g727/kjv/tr/0-1/.

[11] *Collins Dictionary*, https://www.collinsdictionary.com/us/dictionary/english/ravening.

What action does Paul specifically instruct the Corinthians to perform? You won't find Paul telling the young church to *counsel* the sin out of the immoral church member faking Christianity. Previously, in 1 Corinthians 5:5, Paul tells the church to hand over the man to Satan for the destruction of the flesh in hopes that he will be saved.

Plainly shown in verses 11–13, Paul doesn't stop with the sin of sexual immorality in so-called brothers but broadens the list of sins. These additional sins are evident in abusers, whether they commit sexual immorality or not. He follows with, "Put away from yourselves the evil person" (NKJV). Note that Paul's straightforward command doesn't include exceptions for marital status.

Let us not forget, Paul does not even consider this evil person a Christian. The evidence of continual wickedness is a clear proof of the abuser's unredeemed state to those who know the character of our God and the changes that follow authentic salvation.

Pray to receive the gift of discernment of spirits to enable you to see the clandestine cruelty of an abuser claiming to be a good Christian. Be observant. This is especially true if you have already been charmed by the abuser's personality, friendliness, finances, and deceptively pious behavior. You will need the Holy Spirit to wash your eyes and open them to the travesty well hidden behind the illusionary charisma shrouded by a sheep suit.

> Wolves can wear sheep's clothing,
> but they can't hide their appetite.
> Pastor Joanna Eldredge

Are we to suspect an abusive situation under every bush? No, of course not. On the other hand, for too long, we in the church have not recognized the abuse under our noses. We have largely failed to come alongside the wounded lamb.

As pastor, you are the under-shepherd of the Lord's sheep. Suppose one of His bleeding, bitten lambs comes to you bleating that the ram she married is really a wolf in sheep's clothing. Your job does not include stroking the wolf while convincing yourself that he couldn't possibly be as bad as the blood indicates. After all, he teaches in lamb school!

Nor does your responsibility include counseling the wolf and the little lamb together on "their problem." In reality, no earthly shepherd puts a wolf and a lamb together in the sheepfold. Attempting to persuade the wolf into acting more like a lamb is laughable. Whether physical or spiritual sheep, the shepherd's job is to stand between the wolf and the lamb!

Your assignment positively doesn't include insisting that the bleeding lamb go back with the wolf to his den. It doesn't include suggesting she only be meek, exercising godly patience while praying to be a better lamb at the same time waiting for the hungry wolf to grow wool!

Remember, you are a sheepherder, not a wolf care-taker. Become proficient in identifying sheep blood. Ask the Holy Spirit to increase your discernment in recognizing wolves and their methods of attack. Boldly defend the lambs in your care!

CHAPTER 4

PARTNERING WITH JESUS

When asking a woman fleeing abuse how we can assist, she may not even know what would be helpful. The bewilderment and fog of trauma engulf her. She's in shock. Disbelief, mourning, fear, the logistics required to care for herself and possibly her children—all are rolling over her like one-hundred-foot waves.

In any church that is biblically sound and carries the heart of Jesus, there should be people willing and capable of filling some needs such as exampled below. Leadership must model, teach, nurture, and encourage the flock to engage in the care of their fellow lamb.

Let us remember that in Matthew 25:34–40, Jesus is speaking to Tribulation survivors as He is setting up His millennial kingdom, but His character and nature never change. When we care for the hungry, thirsty, stranger, naked, sick, and prisoners (perfect descriptions of abuse survivors), we *are* doing it out of our love for Him. What a privilege!

Please read the questions below, really thinking about each. Let yourself feel the vulnerability you might experience if you were in a powerless situation. Ask Jesus what He would have you do as a church, and as individual members, to express His love to any in your church escaping abuse. We often want to help, but just don't know how.

- For God's sake, will I refrain from asking her the belittling question, "Have you prayed about the separation?" Will I compassionately ask, "How can I pray with you?"
- Will I believe she wouldn't do something this drastic without a good reason?
- Will I listen (over and over again) without judging as she processes through the hurt? Processing verbally often helps a woman make decisions.
- Can I help her check her free credit report *early and frequently in the separation*? Financial ruin often includes the abuser secretly opening online credit accounts fraudulently, only in her name. It is easy for him to do. When these surprise bills arrive at her new address, they must be dealt with legally and swiftly! She must call the companies and close the accounts, registering her innocence. If she was married to the perpetrator at the time of the charges, they will probably try to frighten her into assuming the debt. Legal counsel is imperative.
- Can I drive her to court and stand beside her as her knees shake under his penetrating, intimidating, or defiant gaze?
- Will I praise her for her bravery as she stands up for herself against harassment from him or his allies?
- Can I care for her young children while she meets with her lawyer?

- Can I go with her when she meets her lawyer to take notes for her? Such an appointment is information overload! Am I trustworthy to keep what is said confidential?
- Can I help her build a file folder of documentation so everything her lawyer might request is in one location during the mind-boggling stress?
- Can I help her figure out the confusing legal forms or help her find someone who can?
- Will I pray for her and let her know I am standing with her?
- Can I fill a bag of groceries from my own pantry or give a gift card for food or gas, if she is separated and is trying to make it on her own while in transition?
- Can I discreetly press cash into her hand? Poverty is a favorite tool of the abuser.
- Can I take her shopping for clothing, food, or necessities?
- Can I share an item of clothing from my own closet if I can't afford to buy new? Some women escape with nothing.
- Can I put in a good word for her with a potential employer?
- Can I help her figure out a budget if she needs help when she does earn her own money?
- Can I take her to a bank and teach her how to open an account if that life skill has been withheld? *Yes, this happens.*

- Will I help her think of an emergency plan of escape, including "Help Me" code words, if she is still in the process of formulating her getaway?

- Can I keep her prepacked, emergency bag (money, personal items, passport, etc.) at my house so he can't discover it, get suspicious, and prevent her from leaving?

- Will I help her prepare by locating nearby police or fire stations as safe places to go if followed or harassed while driving? Practicing with her will help her function safely if in the middle of a frightening situation. This is like a fire drill.

- Will I quietly hold her while she grieves and cries? *Women together, not mixed gender, unless family.*

- Can I take photos of injuries from physical abuse and keep them safe as potential evidence?

- Can I help her collect and save emails, texts, and screen prints that document the abuse? Can I keep them safe on my phone or computer for her future reference? This is critical if he still has any access to her computer or phone account or she hasn't yet changed all her passwords to something he can't guess.

- Can I open an account for her legal fees in my name but on her behalf, if possible? Can I discretely host an online fundraiser? Good attorneys are expensive. Ask your banker for suggestions. *This is to avoid the abuser demanding half of any donated funds under possible "communal property" regulations. Confidentiality is key.*

- Can I host a private Love Shower to help her start over if she has been forced to leave with virtually nothing? *This is an unimaginable blessing! I repeat, for reasons stated above, depending upon his level of vileness, it might require confidential invitations only given to trusted people to avoid possible harassment the day of the event.*

- Can I get a phone for her on our family account and make arrangements with her to cover her own costs if she was forced to leave her phone behind or if her phone is still attached to his account? If he still has access to the account she uses, he can still track her movements via GPS and ascertain with whom she has had contact.

  ○ *"Jane," an abused and separated wife, opened a new individual phone account separate from "Dick." She used the same provider, phone, and number she retained from when the abuser originated the family account years previously. Even with her own private new account, not only was Dick still able to activate GPS to follow her, but he also called numbers she had called or texted to determine with whom she had communicated. This was reported to Jane by those Dick had contacted.*

  He threatened to close her private cell phone account if she did not do something he demanded. She rightfully refused despite his efforts to manipulate her. He knew that without a cell phone, she would be isolated further and deprived of communication with those who stood with her and her legal counsel. This was similar to the companion tactic he employed when she was still living in the family home. Among his threats was the statement, "I'll take away your cell phone and your car keys."

After decades of marriage, Dick knew all of Jane's personal security information. Jane called the wireless provider and was assured that he could not close her private account. She was unconvinced and called a second time for reassurances because things always go his way. I was present for that call.

He continued to try to control her actions by threatening to disconnect her phone. The third time she called her provider, the representative was in the process of reassuring Jane that Dick could not cancel or close her account. In God's providential timing, the representative gasped and said, "OMG! The account is closing right now!" The rep allowed Dick to complete the process so it appeared that he had succeeded. Then, the rep reopened Jane's account.

Within hours, mutual friends of ours presented Jane with a new phone, on a line under their plan with a different provider but using Jane's same number. Dick had no access to that account! Jane paid her bill to these friends monthly. That is compassionate love in action.

- Can I provide her the use of my answers to security questions, answers I haven't used? He will not know those. Can I help her think up new answers, codes, or passwords that he won't know? (*I've told two women they could use my mother's maiden name as their own since their abusers couldn't know it and I didn't use it often. Mama, now in heaven, would have been honored to help that way!*)

- Will I assure her that despite the abuser's claims, she is not crazy? She is suffering from the cognitive dissonance that the abuser engineered. Complex post-traumatic stress disorder (c-PTSD) is trauma that compounds or accumulates over a long period of time.

- Can I offer her the use of my computer if she doesn't own one? Some evidence must be tracked down online; some forms must be filled out online.

- Can I assure her that she can call me anytime day or night?

- Will I educate others to put aside their preconceived biases?

- Will I gently, but firmly, challenge those often holier-than-thou attitudes that threaten to re-abuse her in her time of desperate need?

- Will I stand up for her if members of her own family, or church, declare they are "neutral"? Neutral = *neutered* where evil is concerned; it is cowardice. Neutral always aids the abuser.

- Will I stand with her if weak church leadership sides with her abuser because it's less messy for them?

- Will I courageously educate my own church leadership if they are ignorant of the tactics abusers employ?
- Will I remind her that she does, indeed, have choices?
- Will I be humble and allow myself to be educated by those who are experienced in the nuances of narcissistic abuse? (Proverbs 11:14—Am I teachable?)
- Can I use my own healing from an abusive marriage to comfort and encourage her?
- Can I invite her (and her children, if applicable) over for meals? If she is living alone, can I send leftovers with her?
- Can I include her in holidays with gifts? This is especially important if she is bereft of family. Abusers often alienate even her birth family. If the abuser has driven her to poverty, she has not likely been granted legal custody of underage children. Therefore, holidays are especially painful.
- Can I help her laugh and relax for an hour?
- Can I make her my family? Even give her a house key? Victims are often refused keys to the house while living with the abuser. Keys say, "I am valuable. I am family. I am welcome." Your house key can also provide an escape to a safe sanctuary, assuming you understand and accept any potential risks that might be posed by the abuser.
- Will I choose to use language such as "Have you *considered*" rather than "You *should*"?
- Will I give wise counsel but still support her in making her own decisions? Decision-making may

be new to her. She may need help seeing other angles of an issue, but she must still make her own decisions. This is important to redevelop her autonomy, as she may have been forbidden from making decisions by her abuser.

- Will I point her back to Jesus if she asks, "Should I get a divorce?" since it is she who is answerable to God for her decisions?
- Will I suggest options, but not be offended if she is afraid or unable to institute my ideas?
- Will I stand up for her in the midst of conversations critical of her and boldly declare, "We don't know the details, so let's stop discussing or judging her and obey Scripture, which condemns gossiping"?
- Can I offer her my extra bedroom while she gets on her feet?
- Will I love her as Jesus does?
- Can my spouse and I model what a healthy God-fearing, spouse-cherishing marriage looks like? Even with all our warts, can we show her our loving commitment to each other and to the Lord? She may not know how to react when kindness is shown to her because it is a foreign concept after being married to an abuser!

For that matter, does this topic bring to mind MY behavior toward my own spouse? Do I need to submit to Jesus and change something? Dare I ask my spouse for an honest assessment of my behavior?

Oh, my compassionate friend, you might be the only one standing between a precious, abused woman and a bottle of pills or a razor blade poised over her wrist. YOU might be the first, or the only one, to hear Jesus command, "Take off her grave clothes, and let her go."

He who has pity on the poor lends to the LORD,
and He will pay back what he has given.
—Proverbs 19:17 NKJV

ETERNAL HOPE

While this book is written to Christians, perhaps it has come into your hands—but you haven't yet trusted in Jesus Christ as your Savior? Oh, He loves you! You can have hope, and peace He gives. You can look forward to eternity with the One Who loves you most! God does require us to come to Him on His terms.

In the simplest form, what are God's terms for salvation?

    a.   Admit that you are a sinner.
    b.   Believe Jesus is Lord.
    c.   Call upon His name.

Do you want a deeper understanding of coming to Him on His terms?

- **Understand** that every person is on their way to hell because we have all sinned. Hell is not annihilation but an eternal, continual dying, as each person who rejected Jesus's sacrifice for them tries to pay the painful price for their sin that can't be paid by a sinful person. We don't have the ability to release ourselves from the judgment: forever dying alone, without God. We cannot pay the price. It

can only be paid by Someone Who has no sin—
Jesus. You can't earn salvation in any way. It is a gift
we must choose to receive *before we die.*

- ◦ **John 3:18** NKJV tells us, "He who believes
  in Him is not condemned; but he who does
  not believe is condemned already, because
  he has not believed in the name of the only
  begotten Son of God."
- ◦ **Romans 6:23** NASB95 tells us, "For the
  wages of sin is death, but the free gift of God
  is eternal life in Christ Jesus our Lord."
- ◦ **Matthew 13:42, 25:30; Mark 9:43, 9:48;
  and Luke 16:19, 16:23**—verses in which
  Jesus gives vivid descriptions of hell.

- ▪ **Believe** that Jesus Christ is the only Son of God
  and loves YOU so much, He didn't want you to
  go to eternal damnation, so he paid the penalty for
  ALL of your sins on the cross.
  - ◦ **John 3:16** NASB95 reads, "For God so loved
    the world that He gave His only begotten
    Son, that whoever *believes* in Him shall not
    perish, but have eternal life."
  - ◦ **Romans 5:6, 8** NASB95 reads, "For while we
    were still helpless (in our sins), at the right
    time Christ died for the ungodly…but God
    shows His love for us in that while we were
    still sinners, Christ died for us."

- ▪ **Believe** that God established Jesus as **the only Way
  by which humans can be saved** from the eternal

consequences of their sin and rebellion. *There is nothing you can contribute.*

- ◦ **Jeremiah 29:13** NKJV reads, "And you shall seek Me, and find Me, when you shall search for Me with all your heart."
- ◦ **John 5:24** NKJV reads, "Most assuredly, I say to you, he who hears My word and believes in Him who sent Me has everlasting life, and shall not come into judgment, but has passed from death into life."
- ◦ **John 14:6** NASB95 tells us, "Jesus said to him, 'I am the way, and the truth, and the life; no one comes to the Father but through Me.'"
- ◦ **Acts 4:12** NASB95 reads, "And there is salvation in no one else; for there is no other name under heaven that has been given among men by which we must be saved."

- ▪ **Confess** that you are a sinner, living a life apart from God who is Holy, and that you need His forgiveness.
  - ◦ **First John 1:8** NASB95 tells us, "If we say that we have no sin, we are deceiving ourselves and the truth is not in us."
  - ◦ **First John 1:9** NASB95 reads, "If we confess our sins, he is faithful and just to forgive us our sins, and to cleanse us from all unrighteousness."
  - ◦ **Romans 3:10** NKJV reads, "As it is written, 'There is none righteous, no, not one.'"

- ○ **Romans 3:23** NKJV tells us, "For all have sinned and fall short of the glory of God."

- Be **genuinely** repentant (turn from your sins) and sorry for the sins that have kept you separated from God.
    - ○ **Second Corinthians 7:10** NASB95 tells us, "For the sorrow that is according to the will of God produces a repentance without regret, leading to salvation."

- God has made it absolutely clear that no one who comes to Him, under His terms, will be refused. God will not reject you because of your race, color, country of origin, your finances, or your previous belief system. If you want Him, He wants you. No matter what your past sins have been (or those of the present or future), God *will* forgive you because He says He will. Salvation is available to everyone who believes in Jesus as their Savior without any exceptions!
    - ○ **John 1:12** NASB95 reads, "But as many as received Him, to them He gave the right to become children of God, even to those who believe in His name."
    - ○ **Romans 10:13** NASB20 tells us, "For everyone who calls on the name of the Lord will be saved."
    - ○ **Second Peter 3:9** NASB95 reads, "The Lord…is patient toward you, not wish-

ing for any to perish, but for all to come to repentance."

- If you have put all your trust for salvation in Jesus, and Jesus only, tell Him. Talk to Him. Jesus wants to hear your voice!
  - **Romans 10:9, 10** NASB95 tell us, "If you confess with your mouth Jesus as Lord, and believe in your heart that God raised Him from the dead, you will be saved; for with the heart a person believes, resulting in righteousness, and with the mouth he confesses, resulting in salvation."

In your own words, you can tell Him something like this: "Jesus, I am a sinner, but I believe You died and paid the penalty for my sins so that I could live with You forever. Forgive my sins and teach me to live in a way that pleases You. From this day forward I give you my heart, my life, my everything. Thank you for loving me! I receive You now as my Savior and my Lord. Amen."

  - **Luke 15:10** NASB95 reads, "I tell you, there is **joy** in the presence of the angels of God over one sinner who repents."

If you prayed to receive Jesus, you are now a part of the family of God! Look for a church to regularly attend that teaches the Bible and how to become like Jesus, not social justice or "be your best self." Read the Bible every day; start in the Gospel of John. These versions are easy to read and trustworthy: New American Standard Bible (NASB), New King James Version (NKJV), or the English Standard Bible (ESV). All are available in stores or online at https://www. blueletterbible.com or https://www.biblegateway.com and other Bible websites.

I would love to hear that you accepted Jesus or a short testimony of how this little book helped you. However, I am not a counselor; therefore, I will not counsel nor give advice. Please search for a licensed counselor local to you.

Messages received at lazarusrises2024@gmail.com

REFERENCES

The author does not claim to support every opinion in the resources named but has found them to bring enough truth to be of value. These are but a sprinkling of the information on domestic abuse/violence available on the Internet. Please avail yourself of additional instruction.

Books

Crippen, Jeff and Anna Wood. 2012. *A Cry for Justice: How the Evil of Domestic Abuse Hides in Your Church.* South Carolina: Calvary Press.

Crippen, Jeff and Rebecca H. Davis. 2015. *Unholy Charade: Unmasking the Domestic Abuser in the Church.* Oregon: Justice Keepers Publishing.

Ruth, Peggy Joyce. 2002. *Psalm 91: God's Shield of Protection.* Kairos Printing and Production. *Peggy Joyce Ruth is a retired pastor, author, teacher, and conference speaker and one of my dearest friends! Many of her teachings are available on her website or in YouTube:* https://www.peggyjoyceruth.org/ *and* https://www.youtube.com/watch?v=GUHcq5zvfHw&t=13s.

Sampson, Steve. 2003. *Confronting Jezebel: Discerning and Defeating the Spirit of Control.* Bloomington: Chosen Books.

Videos or Websites

Morris, Robert. n.d. "The Jezebel Spirit." https://www. youtube.com/watch?v=jthXLmVtnVI&ab_channel=gatewaychurchtv. *The Jezebel spirit is quite active in narcissistic abuse. Steve Sampson's book listed above is the perfect companion to this video.*

Knowlton, Helena. n.d. "Spiritual Abuse and Lies." https://www.confusiontoclaritynow.com/resources. *Disclaimer:* Lazarus *began as simply a two-page article published on a blog about abuse. It was well received as evidenced by the many encouraging comments from women hurting in or healing from domestic abuse* (https://cryingoutforjustice.blog/2016/08/19/im-nobody-special-what-can-i-do-to-help-lazarus/). *In early 2021, under the Holy Spirit's direction, I augmented my original 2016 article as I felt He wanted it expressed. I began handing out home-printed copies in mid-2021. I've now been asked to make Lazarus available to the public. Thus, in the early fall of 2022, I began editing for publication. I was pleased to discover Helena Knowlton's blog, "Confusion to Clarity Now," on November 2, 2022, and have included her link as yet another resource. No part of "Lazarus" was influenced by Ms. Knowlton's writings in any way.*

Washington County, Oregon, Victim Assistance. n.d. "12 Reasons Why Couple's Counseling Not Recommended

When Domestic Violence Present." https://www.wash-ingtoncountyor.gov/documents/12-reasons-why-cou-ples-counseling-not-recommended-when-domes-tic-violence-present/download?inline. *Succinct points are referenced that validate the abuse victim's legitimate fear of counseling with her controlling abuser in the room. This document justifies her refusal of joint sessions in favor of her right to private, confidential counseling for her own safety. She intimately knows more than you do about the danger she faces!*

I honestly believe that the above links should be considered *required viewing or reading* for every person meeting with couples for premarital, marriage, or family counseling, especially senior staff members. Domestic abuse is far more frequent in churches than most leadership recognizes. Abusers like their tactics to go unrecognized.

Beacham, Russ and Meka Beacham. n.d. "It's Not Love, It's Evil." https://youtu.be/2Ygzlqm0K68 (join in progress at one hour).

Evans, Jimmy. n.d. "Do you have a Jezebel Spirit?" https://youtu.be/ZOjGjc4d5yc.

———. n.d. "Breaking the curse of control." https://youtu.be/nihqCdGagRE.

Grudem, Wayne PhD. n.d. "Reversal of position on divorce." https://www.waynegrudem.com/grounds-for-divorce-why-i-now-believe-there-are-more-than-two.

Murphy, Nancy MD. n.d. "If I were an abuser, what church would I want to attend?" https://andrewjbauman.com/abuserchurch/.

Relevant Magazine. n.d. "Patriarchy and Domestic Abuse." https://www.relevantmagazine.com/faith/church/3-ways-womens-equality-can-counteract-abuse/.

Rohrbaugh, Jamie. n.d. "Jezebel and Prophets." https://www.charismanews.com/opinion/77477-6-differences-between-the-jezebel-spirit-and-true-prophecy.

https://www.charismanews.com/opinion/77524-5-more-differences-between-the-jezebel-spirit-and-true-prophecy. *This is additional teaching regarding the genderless Jezebel spirit in operation in self-appointed prophets. While Ms. Rohrbaugh limits her focus to prophets, this spirit especially operates in abusers who can often be in positions of spiritual leadership. The author knows of three.*

YouTube. "Pastor's ex-wife's story of abuse—testimony full of wisdom and hope." https://www.youtube.com/watch?v=Tdg0umt3UWw&ab_channel=Silently-Bleeding%3AHopeforthePastor%E2%80%99sWife.

NOTES

Raised in the Assemblies of God, Harriet accepted Jesus as her Savior at age five. Her introduction into the predicament of women in domestic abuse began in the early 2000s. So much was learned through the eyes and experiences of these precious women over the years! Early on, Harriet understood the Lord wanted her to share what He placed in her heart so that others might benefit.

For the past fifty years, she has been serving in various positions within Foursquare churches in Oregon, Washington, and, most recently, Florida. Since their marriage in the early 1980s, Harriet has been the blessed wife of Rick, a prior service US Marine and faithful follower of Christ. Together they minister in their South Pasadena church in several capacities, including worship and prayer. God's gift to her of Rick fulfilled her lifelong dream of being a wife, mother, and now grandmother. They are parents to three wonderful adult children and delighted grandparents to five of the greatest grandchildren in the world!

Milton Keynes UK
Ingram Content Group UK Ltd.
UKHW011108150524
442746UK00003B/128